Journal

UNMASK

STOP HIDING START LIVING

Atlanta | Punta del Este

Published by Skinny Brown Dog Media

Atlanta | Punta del Este

www.SkinnyBrownDogMedia.com

Distributed by Skinny Brown Dog Media

Design and composition by Skinny Brown Dog Media

Cover Design by Skinny Brown Dog Media

Library of Congress Cataloging-in-Publication Data Print

UNMASK: Stop Hiding and Start Living

Journal UNMASK: Stop Hiding and Start Living

eBook ISBN: 978-1-957506-38-8

Hardback ISBN: 978-1-957506-39-5

Paperback ISBN: 978-1-957506-40-1

Companion journal: 978-1-957506-41-8

Introduction

Hello Dear One,

In writing UNMASK: Stop Hiding Start Living, it was important for me to share with you the necessary keys to empower your success on this journey, and this journal is just one of them. In this journal, you will find words to empower and inspire you. Journaling was so influential on my road to my healing, a safe place to unmask and begin to move me out of hiding to start living freely. I want you to consider this journal your safe place.

When we go through life wearing masks, it's about image and hiding who we are and what we feel. Masking keeps the pain locked inside, unhealed, festering, and growing.

It was when I could break free of my mask and step into myself that I could start the healing process.

What I discovered as I journaled and started to heal was a space where my truth lived, and that truth was that I was remarkable and that I could choose to live into that remarkable me.

I hope and pray that this journal becomes a place for you to breathe and discover you are remarkable.

Journey well, precious one... ♡
I am praying for you and cheering you on.
Love Wendy

A brief guide on how best to use journal

I believe that the power of journaling has such a profound impact. It has been proven to have immense benefits when you write in a journal; it improves your mental health, which improves your physical health. This is because our mind and body are connected. The body often mimics the state of your mind.

Each one of us will journal differently. Some will write more, and some will write less. There is no right or wrong way.

As you read through *UNMASK: Stop Hiding Start Living* at the end of each chapter, you will find ABC journal prompts:

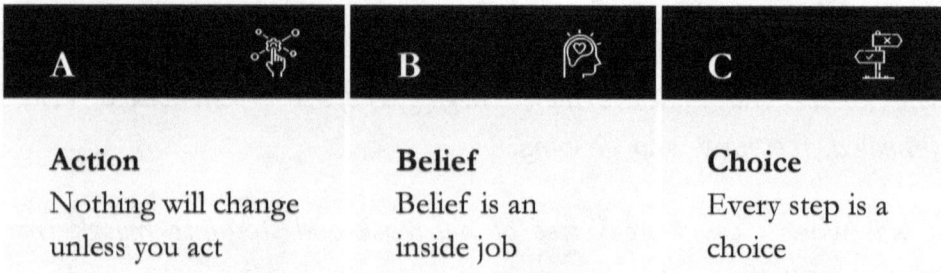

A	**B**	**C**
Action	**Belief**	**Choice**
Nothing will change unless you act	Belief is an inside job	Every step is a choice

Let me encourage you as you journal to dig deep as you answer the prompts. This is where your actions, belief, and choices begin.

In the back of your journal, you will find a space to note your growth moments, those significant steps that keep propelling your forward. It is always empowering to come back and read these when we need a boost on your momentum on the journey.

Let me remind you again this is your safe place to find your truth, work through your moments of forgiveness, know your beliefs, and empower your choices. ♡

I choose to know that I am able

I choose to know I that have brave belief

I choose to know that I have the courage to make better choices

I choose to know that I am worthy of a different life

I choose to know that despite my circumstance, my past, and my age, I will impact and change my future.

I chose to know that if I hang onto my marks, labels, wounds, and memories, I will miss out on the great future that waited for me, the one that I was created to be.

I choose to know that if I let go of the past, my hands will be free to hold all the good things and gifts that God has for me.

I choose to let my self-protection down and trust this unknown God

DATE:

M T W T F S S

Words to guide you:

"

We can choose to turn our tears, our wounds, and our traumas into the courage to walk in hope, to walk into healing victory.

– WENDY

My Daily Notes

DATE:

M T W T F S S

Words to guide you:

❝

Hope is an inside job

– WENDY

Today I Choose...

My Daily Notes

DATE:

M T W T F S S

Words to guide you:

Let your dreams be bigger than your fears and your actions louder than your words.

– CHRISTINE CAINE

Today I Choose...

My Daily Notes

DATE:
_____

M T W T F S S

Words to guide you:

"

We can choose to give power to hopelessness by making choices that let the past influence our present and create a future without hope, or we can choose to power our hope by making choices that enable the remarkable within.

– WENDY

Today I Choose...

My Daily Notes

DATE:

M T W T F S S

Words to guide you:

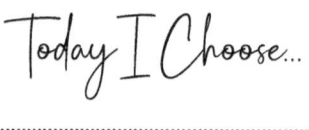

The most important point is, know there is always a way forward, always a choice, a choice for life itself and always a hope for the future

– WENDY

Today I Choose...

My Daily Notes

DATE:

M T W T F S S

Words to guide you:

"

Until we choose to deal with our yesterday today, we're never going to step into tomorrow.

– CHRISTINE CAINE

Today I Choose...

My Daily Notes

DATE:

M T W T F S S

Words to guide you:

What you agree with, you empower; what you empower devours you.

– WENDY

Today I Choose...

My Daily Notes

DATE:

M T W T F S S

Words to guide you:

"

Action creates ownership.

– WENDY

Today I Choose...

My Daily Notes

DATE:
_____

M T W T F S S

Words to guide you:

"

A commitment to growth is a commitment to risk, courage, faith, strength, hope and a willingness to make mistakes, get back up and try again.

– CHRISTINE CAINE

Today I Choose...

My Daily Notes

DATE:

M T W T F S S

Words to guide you:

❝

When we stay trapped behind our masks to the point of losing any sense of the truth of who we are, the only way free is to drop the mask to allow the unmasking to begin.

– WENDY

Today I Choose...

My Daily Notes

DATE:
_____

M T W T F S S

Words to guide you:

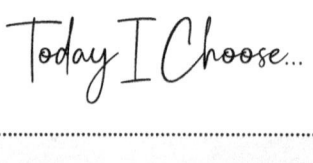

I know you will never see the glory of the other side, the outcome you desire, unless you endure the uphill climb.

– WENDY

Today I Choose...

My Daily Notes

DATE:

M T W T F S S

Words to guide you:

"

Growth requires struggle. The more you are willing to struggle
with your steps, the greater the outcome. Look at how a
caterpillar struggles to emerge from a crystallise to become the
most beautiful remarkable butterfly it was always meant to be.
So it will be with you.

– WENDY

Today I Choose...

My Daily Notes

DATE:
_____

M T W T F S S

Words to guide you:

"

Healing is not always a simple fix and not always a one-and-done event. Healing takes time, and it will look different for everyone.

– WENDY

[   ]

My Daily Notes

DATE:
_____

M T W T F S S

Words to guide you:

"

The biggest achievements are made one step at a time. I want to encourage you to keep going with each and every brave, courageous step.

– WENDY

Today I Choose...

My Daily Notes

DATE:

_____

M T W T F S S

Words to guide you:

"

Keep going, keep getting back up, and each time you will feel stronger.

– WENDY

Today I Choose...

My Daily Notes

DATE:

M T W T F S S

Words to guide you:

"

We have no power to stop the knockdowns, BUT we do have the power to choose to get back up and to know the truth of who we are. Remember staying power is key!

– WENDY

My Daily Notes

DATE:

M T W T F S S

Words to guide you:

"

Let this hope of a better future give you the strength and courage you need to work through the pain and hurt, not just to survive your past, BUT to live victoriously in the present.

– WENDY BURNS

Today I Choose...

My Daily Notes

DATE:

M T W T F S S

> **Life is too short, the world is too big, and God's love too great to live ordinary.**
>
> **– CHRISTINE CAINE**

Today I Choose...

My Daily Notes

DATE:

M T W T F S S

Words to guide you:

"

Never give up, for that is just the place and time when the tide will turn.

- HARRIET BEECHER STOWE

Today I Choose...

My Daily Notes

DATE:

M T W T F S S

Words to guide you:

"

Courage is like a door inside each of us. It's a door with a knob only on the inside, a door that only we can open for ourselves.

– WENDY

Today I Choose...

My Daily Notes

DATE:
_____

M T W T F S S

Words to guide you:

"

Hope has two beautiful daughters; their names are Anger and Courage. Anger at the way things are, and Courage to see that they do not remain as they are.

– AUGUSTINE OF HIPPO

Today I Choose...

My Daily Notes

DATE:
_____

M T W T F S S

Words to guide you:

66

My first step was my step into life. Each step required me to dig deep into my courage. The more I dug for courage, the more I found. Step by step, moment by moment.

— **WENDY**

Today I Choose...

My Daily Notes

DATE:
_____

M T W T F S S

Words to guide you:

"

If the light that is on you is brighter that the light that is in you,
the light that is on you will destroy you.

– CHRISTINE CAINE

Today I Choose...

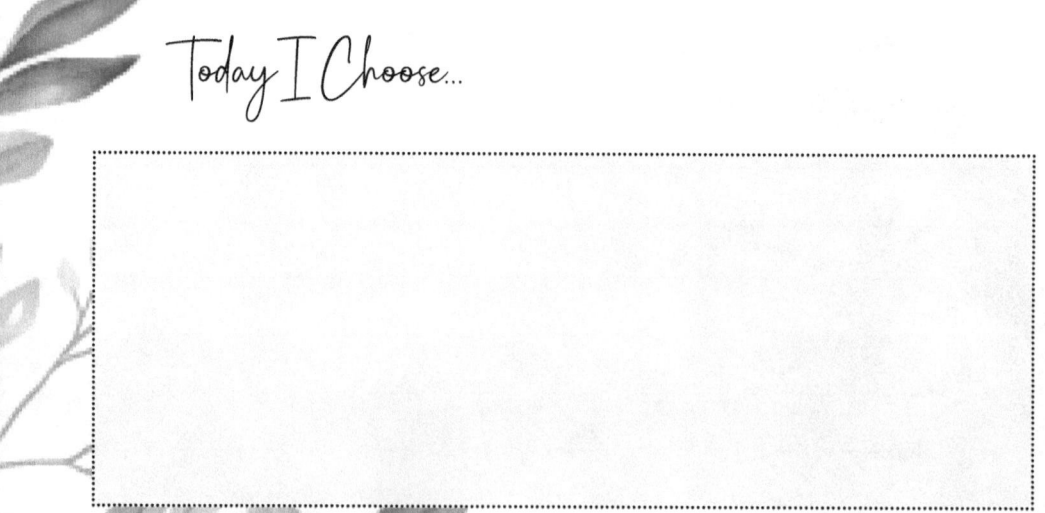

My Daily Notes

DATE:

M T W T F S S

Words to guide you:

"

What's in our hearts will impact our thoughts, beliefs, and words and play out in our actions.

– WENDY

Today I Choose...

My Daily Notes

DATE:

M T W T F S S

Words to guide you:

"

Your legacy, your mark, your fingerprints on the future are
determined by the decisions you make.

– ANDY STANLEY

Today I Choose...

My Daily Notes

DATE:

M T W T F S S

Words to guide you:

"

That the Lord heals the brokenhearted and binds up their wounds and He heals the wounds of every shattered heart.

– PSALM 147:3

Today I Choose...

My Daily Notes

DATE:

M T W T F S S

Words to guide you:

"

Unforgiveness keeps us in an excuses mood, always blaming someone else.

– WENDY

Today I Choose...

My Daily Notes

DATE:

M T W T F S S

Words to guide you:

Forgiveness starts here. Forgiveness liberates the soul. It removes fear. That is why it is such a powerful weapon. The past is the past. We look to the future.

– NELSON MANDALA

Today I Choose...

My Daily Notes

DATE:

M T W T F S S

Words to guide you:

"

Let's not forget that the little emotions are the great captains
of our lives, and we obey them without realizing it.

– VINCENT VAN GOGH

Today I Choose...

My Daily Notes

DATE:

M T W T F S S

Words to guide you:

❝

Pay attention to the welfare of your innermost being, for from there flows the wellspring of life.

— **PROVERBS 4:23**

My Daily Notes

DATE:

M T W T F S S

Words to guide you:

"

In order to move on, you must understand why you felt what you did and why you no longer need to feel it.

— MITCH ALBOM

Today I Choose...

My Daily Notes

DATE:

M T W T F S S

Words to guide you:

"

For as a man thinketh in his heart, so is he.

– PROVERBS 23:7

Today I Choose...

My Daily Notes

DATE:
_____

M T W T F S S

Words to guide you:

"

If you will change, everything will change for you.

– JIM ROHAN

Today I Choose...

My Daily Notes

DATE:
_____

M T W T F S S

Words to guide you:

❝

If you erase all the mistakes of your past, you would erase all
the wisdom of your present. Remember the lesson, not the
disappointment.

– ANONYMOUS

Today I Choose...

My Daily Notes

DATE:

M T W T F S S

Words to guide you:

"

Let the inner movement of your heart always be to love one another, and never play the role of an actor wearing a mask

—ROMANS 12:9

Today I Choose...

My Daily Notes

DATE:

M T W T F S S

Words to guide you:

❝

Experience is not the best teacher; evaluated experience is. You get to decide if that experience is good or bad. Fear of the future or the unknown is a natural response. Confidence comes from having a go and evaluating that experience.

– WENDY

Today I Choose...

My Daily Notes

DATE:

M T W T F S S

Words to guide you:

66

Words kill, words give life; they wither poison or fruit – you choose.

– KING SOLOMON

Today I Choose...

My Daily Notes

DATE:

M T W T F S S

Words to guide you:

"

Joy is the heartbeat of the kingdom of God; Joy is what sustains us; It is our strength. We can be resilient; We can be filled with the expectation of good things.

– WILD AT HEART

Today I Choose...

My Daily Notes

DATE:

M T W T F S S

Words to guide you:

"

Don't edit yourself just simply be aware of your emotions and name them.

– JOHN ELDREDGE

Today I Choose...

My Daily Notes

DATE:
_____

M T W T F S S

Words to guide you:

"

Forgiveness is the light that penetrates the dark and frees the heart to leap forward in freedom.

– WENDY

Today I Choose...

My Daily Notes

DATE:

M T W T F S S

Words to guide you:

❝

We are only invisible when people refuse to see us and when we refuse to see ourselves.

– WENDY

Today I Choose...

My Daily Notes

DATE:

M T W T F S S

Words to guide you:

Today I Choose...

My Daily Notes

DATE:

M T W T F S S

Words to guide you:

"

I choose to know that I am enough.

– WENDY

Today I Choose...

My Daily Notes

DATE:

M T W T F S S

Words to guide you:

Each decision you make becomes a permanent part of your story.

– ANDY STANLEY

Today I Choose...

My Daily Notes

DATE:

M T W T F S S

Words to guide you:

"

Truth is, we don't know what hangs in the balance of our decisions.

– ANDY STANLEY

Today I Choose...

My Daily Notes

DATE:

M T W T F S S

Words to guide you:

“

Be strong. Take courage. Don't be intimidated. Don't give them a second thought because God, your God, is striding ahead of you. He's right there with you. He won't let you down; he won't leave you.

– THE MESSAGE

Today I Choose...

My Daily Notes

DATE:

M T W T F S S

Words to guide you:

"

Then you will experience for yourselves the truth, and the truth will free you

– JOHN 8:32 (B)

Today I Choose...

My Daily Notes

DATE:

M T W T F S S

Words to guide you:

"

Be strong and courageous in every place you step foot.
– CHRISTINE CAINE

Today I Choose...

My Daily Notes

DATE:
_____

M T W T F S S

Words to guide you:

"

When people do not feel heard, they become alienated, even from their soul.

— **RICHARD BLACKABY, BOB ROYALL**

Today I Choose...

My Daily Notes

DATE:
_____

M T W T F S S

Words to guide you:

"

Let go of who you think you are supposed to be and embrace
who you are.

– BRENÉ BROWN

Today I Choose...

My Daily Notes

DATE:

M T W T F S S

Words to guide you:

"

Remember your attitude is one thing you can always control, and it will be the difference maker in your story!

– WENDY

Today I Choose...

My Daily Notes

DATE:

M T W T F S S

Words to guide you:

"

Success is not final, and failure is not fatal: it is the courage to continue that counts.

– WINSTON S. CHURCHILL

Today I Choose...

My Daily Notes

DATE:

M T W T F S S

Words to guide you:

"

Regret is a living power that torments us and reminds us of a pain – It takes courage to face it every time.

– WENDY

Today I Choose...

My Daily Notes

DATE:
_____

M T W T F S S

Words to guide you:

"

Keep your thoughts continually fixed on all that is authentic and real, honorable and admirable, beautiful and respectful, pure and holy, merciful and kind.

– PHILIPPIANS 4:8

Today I Choose...

My Daily Notes

DATE:

M T W T F S S

Words to guide you:

"

Thoughts = Emotions = Actions = Results.

– WENDY

Today I Choose...

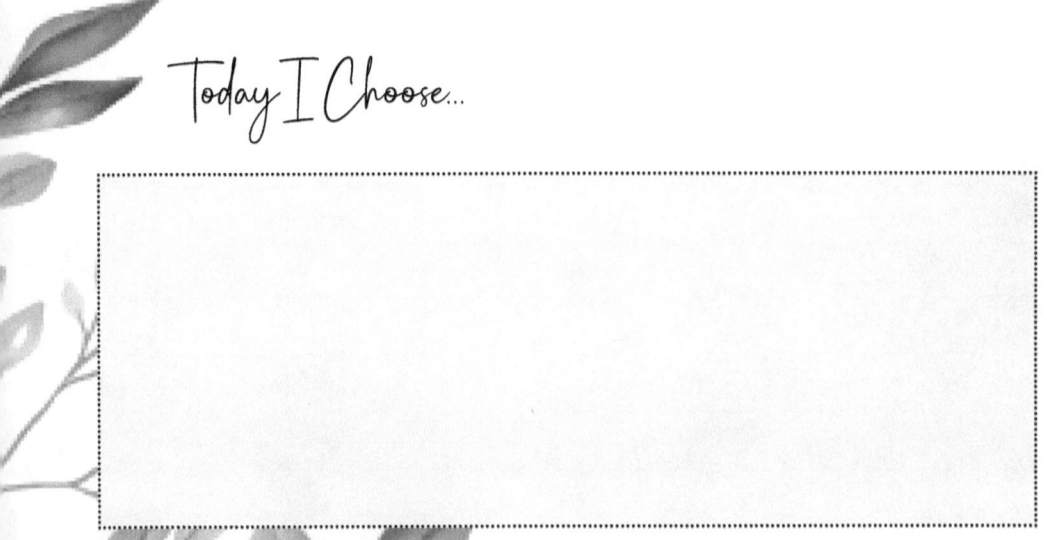

My Daily Notes

DATE:

M T W T F S S

Words to guide you:

"

Harmful self-talk can destroy the potential in each of us and prevent us from living fully in our destiny.

– WENDY

Today I Choose...

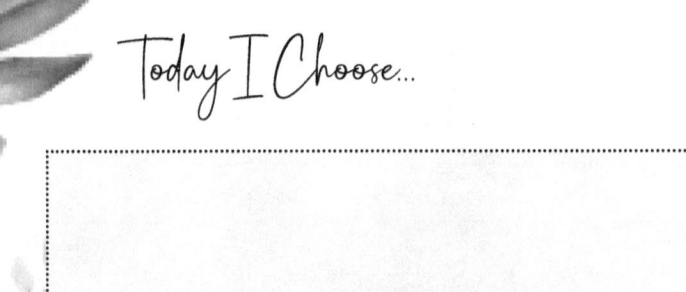

My Daily Notes

DATE:

M T W T F S S

Words to guide you:

66

God is able to take the mess of our past and turn it into a message. He take the trials and tests and turns them into a testimony.

– CHRISTINE CAINE

Today I Choose...

My Daily Notes

DATE:

M T W T F S S

Words to guide you:

"

You are so intimately aware of me, Lord. You read my heart like an open book, and you know all the words I'm about to speak before I even start a sentence! You know every step I will take before my journey even begins. You've gone into my future to prepare the way, and in kindness, you follow behind me to spare me from the harm of my past. You have laid your hand on me!

– PSALM 139:3-5.

Today I Choose...

My Daily Notes

DATE:

M T W T F S S

Words to guide you:

"

Self-care isn't about self-indulgence. It's about refreshing, rehydrating, and renewing our minds, bodies, souls, and spirits for this journey.

– WENDY

My Daily Notes

DATE:

M T W T F S S

Words to guide you:

"

To step into tomorrow's possibilities, you must let go of yesterday's realities. Be careful of your choices between what was, is, and will be. It is tough to fully step into your destiny while you are still holding onto your history.

— **CHRISTINE CAINE**

Today I Choose...

My Daily Notes

DATE:

M T W T F S S

Words to guide you:

"

Joy is a specific defiant choice.

– WENDY

Today I Choose...

My Daily Notes

DATE:

M T W T F S S

Words to guide you:

"

Sometimes being a person of joy amidst our circumstances may seem impossible. It did for me until I took a stand on my journey to say, let the impossible commence.

– WENDY

Today I Choose...

My Daily Notes

DATE:

M T W T F S S

Words to guide you:

"

The power of choice is in your hands. The choice for the courage to walk fully into your destiny for anything to change. Sometimes that courage may simply be getting out of bed and not giving up. *Each time you look fear in the eye and say, 'I see you and step past it,' that's another courageous step forward on your journey.*

My Daily Notes

DATE:

M T W T F S S

Words to guide you:

"

Now is the time for your victory… this is your time… this is your moment!

– WENDY

Today I Choose…

My Daily Notes

Use these last few 'Notes' pages in the back of your journal to note your growth moments, those significant steps that keep propelling you forward. It is always empowering to come back and read these when we need a boost on your momentum on the journey.

Notes

Notes

Notes

Notes